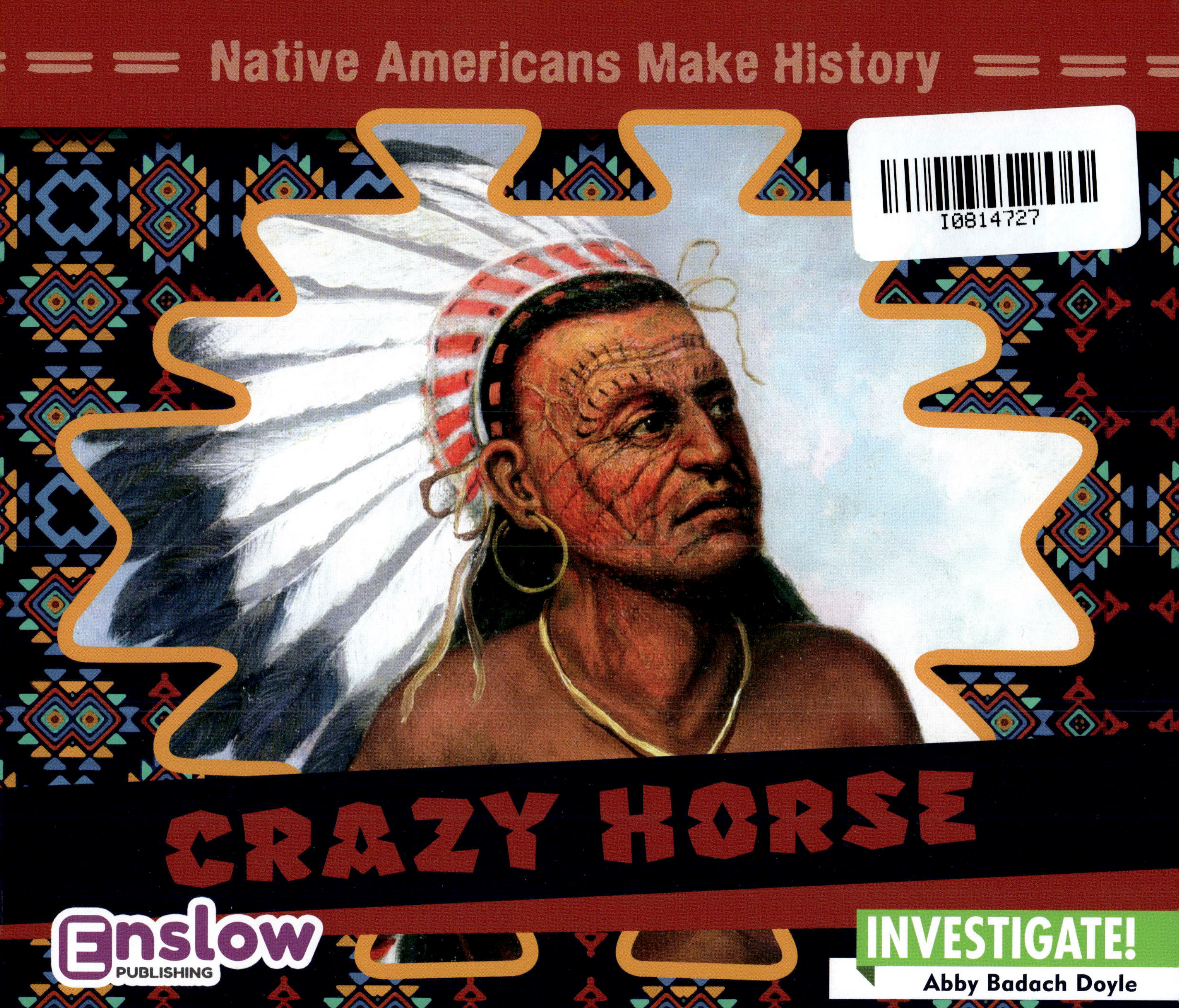
Native Americans Make History
I0814727
CRAZY HORSE
Enslow
PUBLISHING
INVESTIGATE!
Abby Badach Doyle

Please visit our website, www.enslow.com. For a free color catalog of all our high-quality books, call toll free 1-800-398-2504 or fax 1-877-980-4454.

Library of Congress Cataloging-in-Publication Data
Names: Doyle, Abby Badach, author.
Title: Crazy Horse / Abby Badach Doyle.
Description: New York, NY : Enslow Publishing, [2023] | Series: Native Americans make history | Includes index.
Identifiers: LCCN 2021051371 (print) | LCCN 2021051372 (ebook) | ISBN 9781978527607 (library binding) | ISBN 9781978527584 (paperback) | ISBN 9781978527591 (set) | ISBN 9781978527614 (ebook)
Subjects: LCSH: Crazy Horse, approximately 1842-1877–Juvenile literature. | Oglala Indians–Kings and rulers–Biography–Juvenile literature. | Oglala Indians–History–Juvenile literature. | Indians of North America–Great Plains–Wars–Juvenile literature.
Classification: LCC E99.O3 D69 2023 (print) | LCC E99.O3 (ebook) | DDC 978.004/9752440092 [B]–dc23/eng/20211019
LC record available at https://lccn.loc.gov/2021051371
LC ebook record available at https://lccn.loc.gov/2021051372

Portions of this work were originally authored by Miriam Coleman and published as *The Life of Crazy Horse*. All new material in this edition is authored by Abby Badach Doyle.

Published in 2023 by
Enslow Publishing
29 E. 21st Street
New York, NY 10010

Designer: Leslie Taylor
Editor: Abby Badach Doyle

Photo credits: cover background Dmitriy NDM/Shutterstock.com; cover image ©Chicago History Museum/Bridgemanimages.com; series background (cover and interior, Native American pattern) Dmitriy NDM/Shutterstock.com; series artwork Nevada31/Shutterstock.com; p. 5 https://en.wikipedia.org/wiki/File:CrazyHorse.jpg; p. 5 ©Chicago History Museum/Bridgemanimages.com; p. 7 George Catlin (artist)/Bridgemanimages.com; p. 7 stas11/Shutterstock.com; p. 9 Mzorin/Shutterstock.com; p. 9 (inset) https://commons.wikimedia.org/wiki/File:Vapour_baths_of_North_American_Indians._Wellcome_L0005414.jpg; p. 11 https://commons.wikimedia.org/wiki/File:Crazy_Horse_in_War_Paint.jpg; p. 11 (hawk) Brent Simon/Shutterstock.com; p. 13 https://commons.wikimedia.org/wiki/File:Marvels_of_the_new_West_-_a_vivid_portrayal_of_the_stupendous_marvels_in_the_vast_wonderland_west_of_the_Missouri_River_-_comprising_marvels_of_nature,_marvels_of_race,_marvels_of_enterprise,_marvels_(14761716841).jpg; p. 13 (prospector) https://commons.wikimedia.org/wiki/File:Prospector_with_shovel_and_gold_pan_at_the_edge_of_a_creek,_Yukon_Territory,_ca_1898_(MEED_158).jpg; p. 13 (gold dust) https://commons.wikimedia.org/wiki/File:Gold_dust_(placer_gold)_2_(16849889230).jpg; p. 15 (map) https://commons.wikimedia.org/wiki/File:Bozeman01.png; p. 15 Harper's Weekly, v. 11, no. 534/LOC.com; p. 17 https://commons.wikimedia.org/wiki/File:America,_Native_North_American,_Central_Plains,_Lakota_Sioux,_19th_century_-_Hide_Shirt_-_1984.1046_-_Cleveland_Museum_of_Art.tif; p. 19 The Picture Art Collection/Alamy.com; p. 21 (Black Hills) Wollertz//Shutterstock.com; p. 21 (Sitting Bull) https://commons.wikimedia.org/wiki/File:Sitting_Bull,_Notman.jpg; p. 21 (Gall) https://commons.wikimedia.org/wiki/File:Chief_Gall.png; p. 23 https://commons.wikimedia.org/wiki/File:Sioux_charging_at_Battle_of_Rosebuddenver.jpg; p. 23 (inset), 25 Everett Collection/Shutterstock.com; p. 27 https://commons.wikimedia.org/wiki/File:Crazy_horse_c1877.jpg; p. 27 (memorial marker) https://commons.wikimedia.org/wiki/File:Ftrob_ch.JPG; p. 29 (protest) arindambanerjee/Shutterstock.com; p. 29 (monument) https://commons.wikimedia.org/wiki/File:Crazy_Horse_up_close.jpg.

Printed in the United States of America

CPSIA compliance information: Batch #CSENS23: For further information contact Enslow Publishing, New York, New York, at 1-800-398-2504.

CONTENTS

Words in the glossary appear in **bold** type the first time they are used in the text.

A BRAVE FIGHTER

Crazy Horse was a brave Lakota warrior. He famously fought boldly in the Battle of the Little Bighorn in 1876. Here, he led Lakota and Cheyenne warriors as they defeated, or beat, the U.S. Army.

Crazy Horse never had his picture taken. His life lives on through stories that were passed down over time. We may never know some facts or dates for sure. We know what likely mattered most to him, though. Crazy Horse believed Native People should live on the land they find **sacred**. He fought hard to protect, or keep, that right.

Crazy Horse

The Crazy Horse Memorial will be the world's largest mountain monument. Only his face is finished, but the work continues little by little.

Explore More!

In 1948, work began on a giant monument to honor Crazy Horse in South Dakota. When finished, it will stand 563 feet (171.6 m) tall. That's more than twice as tall as the Statue of Liberty, from the top of the base to her torch!

GROWING UP

Crazy Horse was born around 1840, possibly near present-day Rapid City, South Dakota, in the Black Hills. His father, also named Crazy Horse, was a **medicine man**. As a child, he was called "Curly Hair" because his hair was unusually curly.

Crazy Horse grew up traveling the land with the Oglala Lakota people, following bison herds. He also played war and hunting games that became important later in his life. By the age of 10, Crazy Horse was skilled at riding horses and shooting. He even captured and trained his own wild horse.

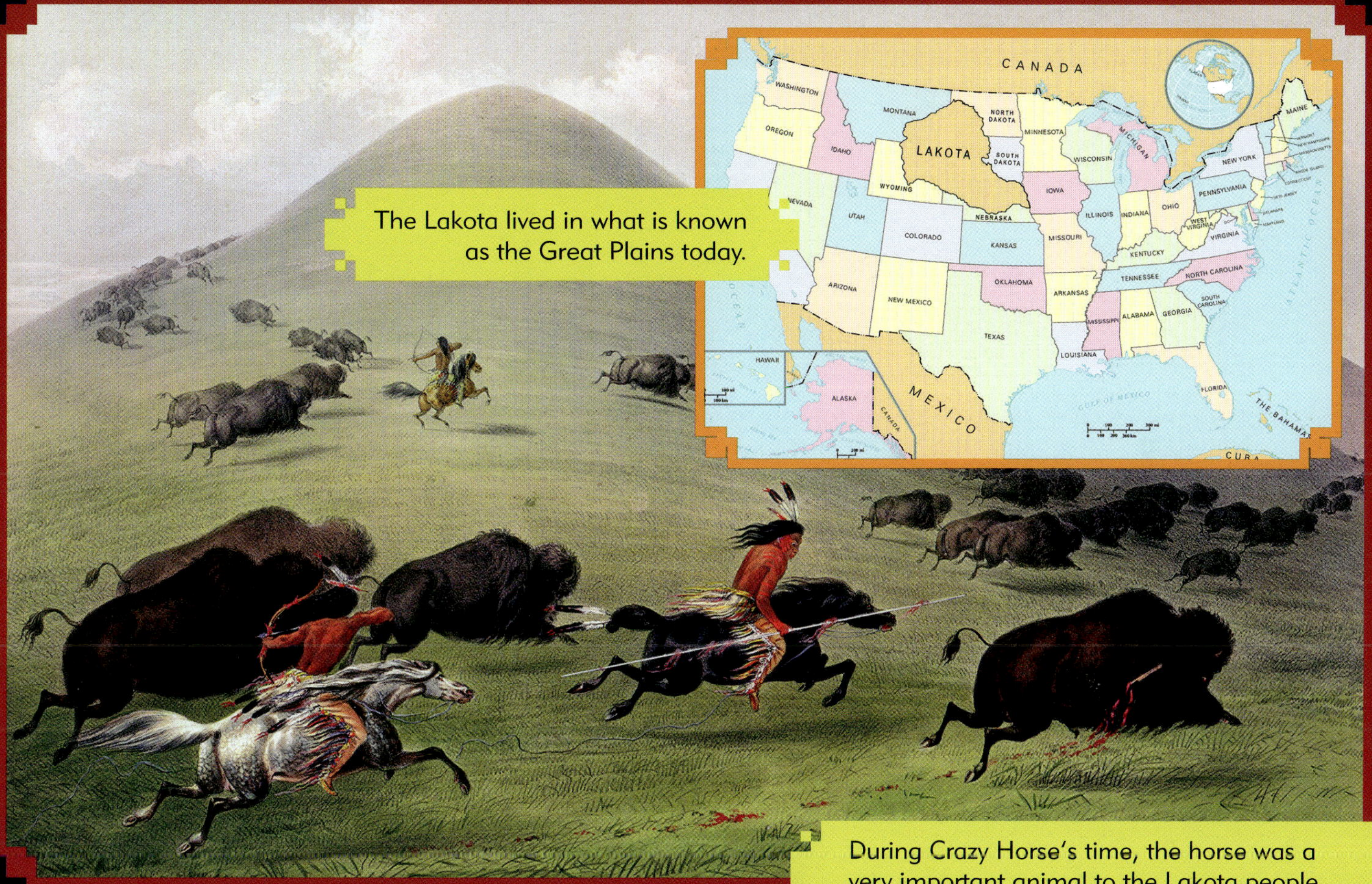

The Lakota lived in what is known as the Great Plains today.

During Crazy Horse's time, the horse was a very important animal to the Lakota people. They rode horses often to travel and hunt.

Crazy Horse's father was from the Oglala band of Lakota. His mother was Miniconjou Lakota. The Lakota people are part of the Great Sioux Nation. Today, some are against the term "Sioux" because it means "little snakes" and was used by their enemies.

ALONE IN THE WILD

At about 14, Crazy Horse was already a brave leader among the other boys. However, he wanted to know what to do when he grew up. He went by himself into nature on a journey for knowledge called a **vision** quest. This was something many young Lakota boys did.

While alone, Crazy Horse had a vision. He saw a man on horseback in a thunderstorm. The man was simply dressed, with a single feather in his hair and a stone behind his ear. Crazy Horse then knew he was meant to be a warrior.

A vision quest was an important step to becoming a Lakota warrior.

Native American sweat lodge

Explore More!

To prepare for a vision quest, the Lakota boys would sit in a sweat lodge. This is a building that is made very hot to make people sweat. Then they would avoid food and water as they prayed for a vision.

The man on horseback was floating and had a bolt of lightning on his cheeks. He told Crazy Horse to toss or rub dust on himself before he rode into a fight. He also said that Crazy Horse should never take anything for himself during a battle.

From then on, Crazy Horse would follow these instructions, or directions, when he fought. He would dress like the man on horseback too. These **symbols** were important to the Lakota people. They believed that **rituals** before battle would give a warrior power and safety.

In his language, Crazy Horse was called Tasunke Witco.

Explore More!

Crazy Horse also saw a hawk flying in his vision. Hawks are fast, powerful hunters. Crazy Horse would sometimes ride into battle with the body of a hawk tied to his head, or just a single feather in his hair.

SETTLERS MOVE WEST

As a young man, Crazy Horse became known as a skilled fighter in battles with other Native American tribes. Beginning in the mid-1800s, white settlers began traveling west in large numbers. Many passed through or settled on Lakota territory. Soon, this would lead to war.

The white settlers wanted Lakota land to build homes, mine for gold, or hunt and trap animals. From the time he was young, Crazy Horse learned not to trust the settlers or U.S. soldiers. As a boy, he saw soldiers shoot a Sioux chief.

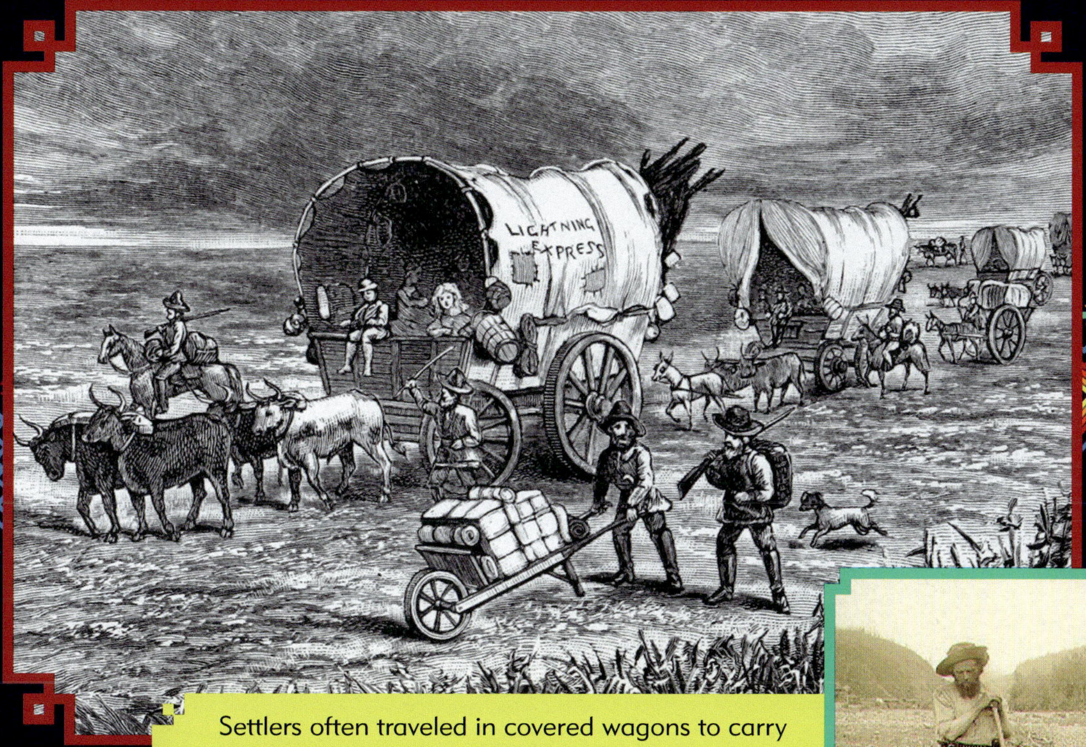

Settlers often traveled in covered wagons to carry their belongings and supplies.

gold dust

Someone who searches the land for valuable matter, such as gold, is called a prospector.

Explore More!

When Crazy Horse was alive, the Lakota people had a lot of power in the northern Great Plains. They got along well with the nearby Cheyenne and Arapaho people. These groups worked together to **defend** their land from white settlers.

FIGHTING FOR LAND

In the 1860s, Crazy Horse joined Oglala warrior Red Cloud who **declared** war against white settlers along the Bozeman Trail. This trail, traveled by white settlers looking for gold, ruined a Lakota hunting ground. Crazy Horse led attacks of soldiers and settlers at settlements and forts. This came to be called Red Cloud's War.

In December 1866, Crazy Horse helped attack Fort Phil Kearny in present-day Wyoming. He drew a troop of U.S. soldiers away from their fort. Then, Lakota, Arapaho, and Cheyenne warriors surprised the soldiers. They killed 81 soldiers.

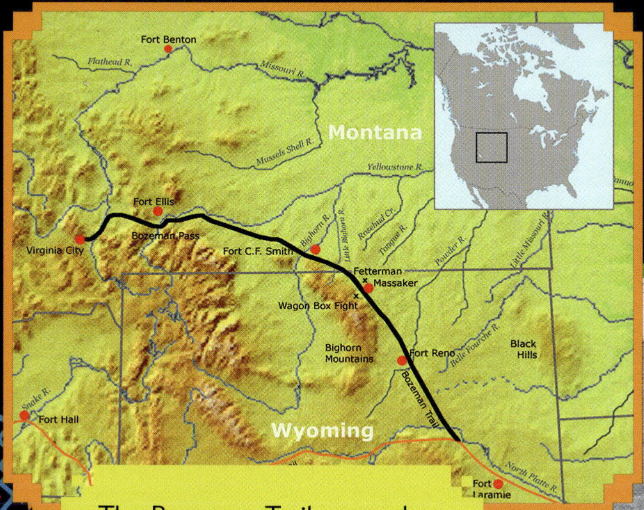

The Bozeman Trail, named for John Bozeman, is located in modern day Montana.

The Fort Phil Kearny attack, shown here, was part of Red Cloud's War.

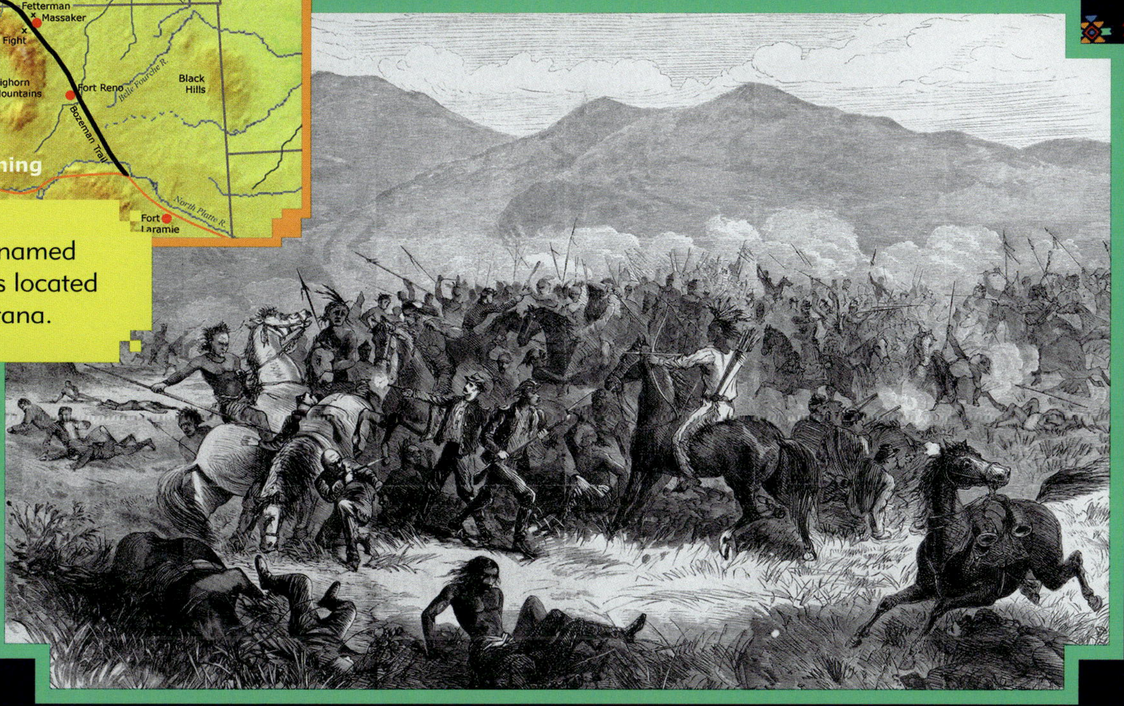

The Fort Phil Kearny attack became known as the Fetterman Massacre. A massacre is the killing of a large number of people, often when they cannot guard themselves. In 1864, U.S. soldiers led a massacre of Southern Cheyenne and Arapaho people in modern-day Colorado.

SHIRT WEARER

In the mid-1860s, around the time of Red Cloud's War, Crazy Horse earned the title of shirt wearer. This was one of the highest Lakota honors. It was given to four Oglala men whose actions showed notable bravery and sacrifice. Sacrifice is when someone gives up something they want to help others.

Shirt wearers were the first men to ride into battle and the last to leave. Shirt wearers had other duties to help the tribe too. As a shirt wearer, Crazy Horse would help his people find campsites and hunting grounds.

This is a Lakota hide shirt. Crazy Horse's shirt may have looked something like this.

Explore More!

As the name suggests, shirt wearers were given special clothing. Oglala Lakota leaders made the shirts using animal hide. They added decorations, like hair and seashells, to each shirt. Each decoration and color meant something special to the Lakota.

A PROMISE OF PEACE

The fighting continued between the Sioux and the U.S. government. In 1868, the two groups signed a treaty, or agreement, at Fort Laramie in present-day Wyoming. The 1868 Treaty of Fort Laramie said the U.S. government would close the Bozeman Trail and its forts in return for peace.

The treaty also created the Great Sioux Reservation. Here, the government would supply the Lakota with seeds, animals, tools, and training to become farmers. Crazy Horse did not support the treaty. He did not want his people to have to live on reservations.

Lakota leaders pose for a picture with U.S. peace commissioners while the two groups meet to go over the 1868 Treaty of Fort Laramie.

Explore More!

A reservation, also called an agency, is land set aside by the U.S. government for Native Americans to live. The Great Sioux Reservation included the Black Hills, or Paha Sapa in the Lakota language, which is sacred Lakota land. The government promised it would belong to them forever.

A FIGHT FOR THE BLACK HILLS

Trouble started again in 1874 when prospectors found gold in the Black Hills. Hundreds of white settlers traveled to the area to get rich. The U.S. Army came to protect the white settlers, even though the Fort Laramie Treaty said this was Sioux land.

In 1875, the U.S. government offered to buy the Black Hills. The Lakota refused, saying the land was not for sale. In reply, the U.S. government ignored the Fort Laramie Treaty and said any Lakota who did not move to a reservation would be considered an enemy.

Chief Gall

Today, the Black Hills are part of Badlands National Park and the Black Hills National Forest.

Explore More!

Around this time, Crazy Horse joined the great Lakota chiefs Sitting Bull and Gall. They led a band of Lakota and Cheyenne people who refused to leave their homeland. In 1876, the U.S. Army began a series of attacks to force them onto reservations.

BATTLE OF THE ROSEBUD

The next summer, many Native Americans led by Sitting Bull camped along Rosebud Creek in what is now Montana. They knew they were disobeying the U.S. government who told them to move to the reservation. On June 17, 1876, General George Crook led more than 1,000 soldiers there to make them move.

While the soldiers took a rest, Crazy Horse surprised them. He had 1,500 Sioux warriors with him. Another 2,500 warriors completed the charge. They fought with great strength to keep their land. Together, the Native Americans stopped Crook and his soldiers.

In 1876, an artist drew this picture of what the Battle of the Rosebud may have looked like.

Chief Sitting Bull

Explore More!

Sitting Bull was a member of the Hunkpapa band of Lakota. He was also a great warrior and leader. Like Crazy Horse, Sitting Bull distrusted white settlers and the U.S. government. He fought to keep the **traditional** Lakota way of life.

LITTLE BIGHORN

More than a week later, thousands of Lakota and Cheyenne people camped along the Little Bighorn River. On June 25, 1876, **Lieutenant Colonel** George Armstrong Custer led hundreds of soldiers there. Sitting Bull, too old for battle, looked after people at the camp. Crazy Horse led a group of warriors to fight.

The U.S. Army was greatly outnumbered. Crazy Horse's daring leadership was important to the battle's result. The Battle of the Little Bighorn is one of the most famous wins for Native Americans. However, it caused the U.S. government to send more troops.

The Battle of the Little Bighorn became known as "Custer's Last Stand."

Explore More!

We may never know exactly how many Native Americans were camped along the Little Bighorn River during this time. Historians say it was likely between 8,000 and 10,000 people. In that group, about 1,500 to 1,800 of them were warriors.

CRAZY HORSE'S DEATH

The U.S. took control of the Black Hills in 1877, but the Sioux people have a legal battle today claiming their ownership. Sitting Bull escaped to Canada. Many Lakota moved to reservations. Crazy Horse kept fighting. In May 1877, Crazy Horse surrendered, or gave up. It was peaceful, but he still did not get along with U.S. Army leaders.

They thought he might attack again, so they tried to take Crazy Horse to jail. On the way, he resisted, or opposed, arrest. In the struggle, a guard wounded him. He died on September 5, 1877.

Crazy Horse surrendered at Fort Robinson, in modern-day Nebraska.

Crazy Horse memorial marker

Explore More!

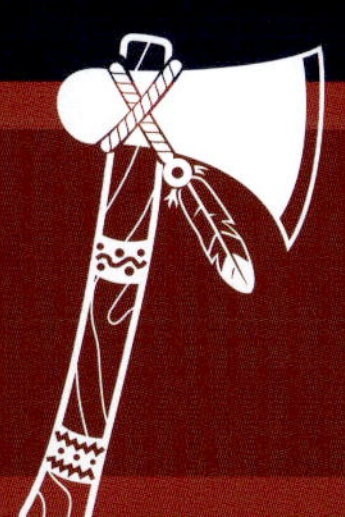

Crazy Horse did not speak English. It was hard for him and the guards to understand each other. It is unclear exactly what happened in the final days of Crazy Horse's life or in the struggle that led to his death.

A STORY LIVES ON

Struggles over Native American land still happen today. In 2016, the Standing Rock Sioux Tribe famously opposed an oil pipeline planned to run underneath their reservation. They said it would pollute water and ruin the land where their **ancestors** were buried. People from around the world joined their peaceful **protest**.

Crazy Horse was a warrior, but he also wanted peace. Crazy Horse once said he believed one day people of all races would join together under the sacred tree of life. Today, people still look to him as an example of bravery and **resistance**.

More than 200 Native American tribes joined to protect land at Standing Rock.

The Crazy Horse Memorial is in South Dakota.

THE LIFE OF CRAZY HORSE

- **circa (around) 1840** – Crazy Horse, known then as Curly Hair, is born in present-day South Dakota.
- **circa 1854** – Crazy Horse experiences his first vision quest.
- **1863** – The Bozeman Trail on Native American land is made wider for more settlers to travel.
- **1865** – Red Cloud starts a war to protest settlement along the Bozeman Trail, which Crazy Horse joined.
- **1868** – The Sioux and the U.S. government sign the Fort Laramie Treaty of 1868.
- **1874** – Prospectors discover gold in the Black Hills.
- **1875** – The U.S. government offers to buy the Black Hills. The Lakota refuse, and the government orders them onto reservations.
- **June 17, 1876** – Crazy Horse defeats U.S. forces at the Battle of the Rosebud.
- **June 25, 1876** – Lakota and Cheyenne forces defeat George Armstrong Custer's forces during the Battle of the Little Bighorn.
- **September 5, 1877** – Crazy Horse surrenders at Fort Robinson, Nebraska. He dies after being wounded by a U.S. soldier.

Explore More!

Korczak Ziolkowski helped carve, or cut stone, for Mount Rushmore in South Dakota. In 1939, Oglala chief Henry Standing Bear asked him to carve the Crazy Horse Memorial. Ziolkowski died in 1982, but his children and grandchildren continue the work today.

GLOSSARY

ancestor: A relative who lived long before you.

declare: To say something in a way that is public or official.

defend: To guard against harm.

lieutenant colonel: A military officer of middle rank.

medicine man: Someone who acted as a healer and spiritual leader in Native American culture.

protest: An event at which a group objects to an idea, an act, or a way of doing something.

resistance: The opposition or prevention of something.

ritual: A formal ceremony.

sacred: Specially blessed.

symbol: A picture, shape, or object that stands for something else.

traditional: Having to do with long-practiced customs.

vision: Something seen by a way other than normal sight, such as in sleep or the imagination.

FOR MORE INFORMATION

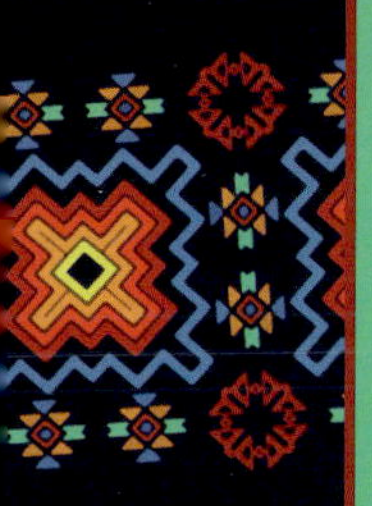

Books

Benson, Jodyanne. *Crazy Horse*. New York, NY: Cavendish Square, 2020.

Nelson, S. D. *Crazy Horse and Custer: Born Enemies*. New York, NY: Abrams Books for Young Readers, 2021.

Strand, Jennifer. *Crazy Horse*. Minneapolis, MN: Abdo Zoom, 2017.

Websites

Crazy Horse
kids.britannica.com/kids/article/Crazy-Horse/353011
Read the facts about Crazy Horse's life on this website just for kids.

Crazy Horse Memorial
crazyhorsememorial.org
Hear the story and see the dream for the giant monument to honor Crazy Horse in South Dakota.

Where Sitting Bull and Crazy Horse Defeated Colonel Custer
learninglab.si.edu/resources/view/246651
Learn more about the Battle of the Little Bighorn in this video from the Smithsonian Institution.

INDEX